'Ta-ra-

CW01081163

A little book of language used by 'Brummies'

By Stephen Burrows & Michael Layton

First Published by Bostin Books February 2018 (Find
us on our Facebook Page 'Bostin Books')

This little book is dedicated to all 'Brummies'
wherever they are. I hope is that it brings back fond
memories, and a smile to the fizzogs of readers.

Introduction

I was inspired to compile this 'bostin' little book by a Facebook post that went 'viral'. The post contained a few Brummie expressions that my co-author, Mike Layton and I, had compiled for authenticity purposes to use in our Birmingham focused novels.

The interest shown was overwhelming. The phrases came from our memories of growing up in the City, with many of them used by us, as well as our parents and grandparents. Just writing down these few words and phrases brought back both memories and laughter.

Mike and I are *'baby boomer'* Brummies, and descendants of several generations of Brummies. Mike lived in Wheeler Street, Lozells, whilst I lived in Moseley for my first twenty-five years. We both still retain the accent and use terms such as *'traffic island'* and *'gambol'* without fully realising their local nature and history – that is until now.

The original post was shared on social media many times and attracted literally hundreds of comments. There was much humour, especially as a number of offspring, friends and family, realised that these funny phrases used by their parents and partners were actually genuine!

Many people asked for a translation and whether a collation of terms could be produced. Here it is!

***

A Word On Origins

This book has been written for fun.

I am not a student of etymology (historical language change), and make no claims of expertise, I have just done my best.

Some of the contents of this book are of Brummie origin, many are from the Black Country, whilst some are involved in an endless tug of war for ownership. Others may come from the Midlands or further afield. This book is **not claiming Birmingham ownership for any of them, just usage.**

In particular, the geographical proximity of Birmingham to the Black Country leaves little doubt that many slang terms originated in the Black Country and have subsequently been given a Brummie pronunciation.

It would take many years of research and expertise in the history of language to definitively trace and locate the origins of the words and phrases – if that were indeed possible.

English /Anglo-Saxon is itself a conglomeration of words from all over the world, especially Scandinavia and Europe, and further back, Latin, so solving the question of ultimate ownership is a fairly pointless and fruitless endeavor.

If you add the fact that the population of the United Kingdom has, since the Industrial Revolution, been highly migratory, particularly from rural villages to the new big cities such as Birmingham, it is not surprising that local language gets moved with the people.

So all this book is claiming, is that these words and phrases were/are in use in Birmingham, and some have been so for a very long time – wherever they originally came from.

In the end, does it matter? The really important thing

is to treasure, preserve, laugh at, and use them. Language is part of our heritage and belongs to us.

***

A Note On Pronunciation

A joke for Brummies:

'What is the difference between a Buffalo and a Bison?' You can only wash your hands in a *'Bison'*.

The Brummie accent is much abused, rarely correctly imitated, full of warmth and humour, and almost impossible to recreate on the page.

Without being spoken, some of the following words and phrases lose their individual Brummie character. I have tried, where possible to indicate pronunciation, but my recommendation is to seek out your oldest living Brummie relative and get them to say them.

As a general rule though, forget any 'H's at the start of words, and 'G's at the end – unless it's *'Garding'* which has the benefit of a bonus 'G' in Birmingham.

I have made a valiant attempt to group the contents as sayings, action words and descriptive words to keep it in some sort of order, some are all three, but it doesn't really matter.

Have fun, *'ere we go!'* (Stephen Burrows 2018)

Figure 1 Me Dad with other engineers at the Land Rover

PART ONE

SAYINGS

Never in the rain/ reign of Pig's Pudding

Let's start with a good one. It means that it will never
happen, whatever it is. It was very widely used in
Birmingham in the past. I cannot find any information
on its origins to date. Pig's Pudding is Black Pudding
but why and whether it rains or reigns is a good
question. Either way, it's not going to happen.

*

*A face like fourpence / a smacked arse / A face as
long as Livery Street*

Someone is looking miserable. There are other local
dialect phrases concerning four- pence and they all
seem to revolve around an item that was too
expensive at four- pence and would be left on the
shelf. Perhaps that made it look miserable, and what
child with a smacked arse looks happy? Livery Street
still exists and is a very long road – oroight?

And whilst we are on the subject of faces....

*

A face like a bosted boot / arse / welder's bench / bag of spanners /rough as a goat's knee

I'm afraid that you are not a pretty sight....Both the rural and industrial influences are clear. Useful descriptions – preferably out of earshot of the subject!

*

Ark at that rain / Ark at er

In true Brummie tradition the 'H' has gone AWOL, (Absent Without Official Leave), in two words, but this is clearly a derivative of the old word 'Hark' as in 'Hark The Herald Angels', but there were clearly other things to listen to in Birmingham, like 'er next door'.

*

Use a Birmingham Screwdriver

My Dad was an engineer and used this phrase all the time. If something gets stuck, hit it with a big hammer. Never fails.....to break something.

*

(Going) All Around The Wrekin

Beating about the bush, not getting to the point. The Wrekin is a big hill in Shropshire and I suspect that the Brums went on day trips out there, before package holidays to Torremolinos became affordable.

*

(It's a bit) Black over Bill's Mother's

It's gonna piss down in a bit Bab. Nottinghamshire folk are adamant that this relates to some farmer up that way, but this saying has been used in Birmingham for generations.

The most likely explanation is that 'Bill's Mother' is Mary Arden, 'Bill' Shakespeare's Mom, and the location is her house in Stratford, which is of course preserved and has been a day trip destination for generations of Brummies. The prevailing weather is supposed to come from that direction, bringing storms.

The saying may go back even further, having been brought to Birmingham by Warwickshire agricultural workers moving to the city during the Industrial Revolution.

This is also the title of a Bostin book by Steve Burrows and Michael Layton. (Got to gerra plug in ain't ya?)

*

(Your mom / sister works at) The back of Rackhams

Your female relative is a lady of the night. This phrase is One Hundred Per Cent Brummie. It is incredible that generations of Brummies know what this means, when any evidence of this place being a red light area is extremely old and vague.

*

Any road up

Anyway, to get to the point of, or return to the original subject of the conversation.... Also, this was the title of Birmingham group, The Steve Gibbon's Band's, first LP, released in 1976 – which shows it was a well-known saying in Birmingham back then.

*

Gerrin on me wick

Annoying me. This is in fact from Cockney Rhyming

slang. Wick is from Hampton Wick, slang for 'prick'. The slang seems to have originated from use by soldiers in World War II.

*

Got a cob on

Annoyed or sulking. Widespread nationally and probably not Brummie in origin, but used in the city.

*

(You look like) A sack of spuds / bag of rags tied round the middle

Your dress sense leaves something to be desired...Probably has agricultural origins, coupled with memories of the urban life of the poor.

*

For the umpteenth time

How many times have I got to tell you? The word 'umpteenth' has an interesting history. An 'umpty' was a slang term originally referring to a Morse Code dash but became the word for an indefinitely large

number. The 'teenth' bit just makes it sound better,
like 'nineteenth'.

*

*Red hat, no drawers / Fur coat no knickers / all
kippers and curtains*

Dresses or acts posh, but really hasn't a 'hapeth' to
rub together.

*

Never in a month of Sundays

It's not happening, it will take forever or I'm not
doing it...Dates back to at least the Eighteenth
Century. Traditionally Sundays were long' boring
days where nothing was open and activity was
limited. A month of Sundays takes about thirty weeks
– seeming like forever.

*

Got a bob on isself

Someone with 'airs and graces', an ego. My Mom
used to call them 'affected' but I've never heard
anyone else use that phrase.

*

Borrow us a ..

A classic Brummie phrase meaning, lend me
something. Why not use 'lend? Who knows or cares,
it's just great.

*

I'll go to the foot of our stairs

I am amazed and surprised. Northern in origin, but
adopted by Brummies generations ago. Probably
something to do with having a walk to recover
equanimity – or even 'I'm off to bed I'm so
surprised'.

*

(We had a) Couple or three

More than two, probably more than three, but not
lots.Originates in the USA, how it got to Birmingham
is anyone's guess.

*

Up and down like a mad woman's knickers or
breakfast / ooers drawers / yo yo / bride's nightie

Just a sample of a very generic and global phrase in English speaking countries, especially Australia. Lots of the alternatives must have specific historical origins. A useful clutch of variations to imbue your conversation with character and get you roundly condemned for being 'un PC' - your choice.

*

Fair to middlin

Feel like I've got an illness coming on. 'Middling' is an old noun that denotes forthcoming illness.

*

Couldn't stop a pig in an entry

Bandy–legged. A Black Country saying used in Birmingham that is too good to leave out - Nuff said.

*

She's bin babbied

The lady is with child.

*

Five and Twenty Past / To

How old Brummies tell the time. Forget digital
displays, this dates back to proper clocks with hands.

*

There and back to see how far it is

The Brummie rejoinder to 'where ya goin?' or,
'where's ya bin?'

*

Put the wood in the hole, were you born in a barn?

Shut the bloody door before the heat gets out and
costs us more money Usually uttered by long-
suffering Dads who had to pay the bills.

*

They'd skin a fart for a ha'penny

Deep pockets, short arms.

*

*Up the wooden hill to Bedfordshire – Down sheet
Lane – and along Blanket Alley*

Get to bed. I only knew the first part, but my
Brummie wife remembered the lot

*

Ee's a right Peaky Blinder / Ee's a little blinder

He's smartly dressed or He's a little monster. From
the 1920's, and we all know about the Peaky Blinders
now. If you want to know more, look out for
Professor Carl Chinn's book, *'The Real Peaky
Blinders'*.

*

What's a marrer? – A cucumbers uncle

Only the genuine Brummie accent can achieve the
pronunciation required to make this 'in joke' work.

*

I don't give a jot nor tickle

Reported as used by older Brummies. Origin obscure,
but the word 'jot' derives from 'iota' the smallest

letter in the Greek alphabet or Hebrew 'Yod' both of which have come to represent nothing. 'Tickle' is likely to refer to being tickled or amused by something – or in this case not.

*

A cat lick and a promise

A cat lick is a perfunctory wash, but the phrase 'a lick and a promise' is very old, dating back at least to the first half of the 1800's, and means something not done properly.

*

Go play up yer own end!

A gentle encouragement for annoying kids playing in the horse road to go and be a nuisance outside their own houses.

*

You'll ave it dark

Gerra move on, its night time in ten hours.

*

This ain't gonna get the babby a new frock/ pinny

What we are doing isn't achieving anything in money terms. We are wasting our time when we could be getting on with something productive. Black Country.

*

It's like New Street Station ere

It's packed innit?

*

Havin the bags on, or Got the bags on

Annoyed about something. I can remember my Gran saying this but can find no reference as to its origins. I wonder if it might relate to menstruation and associated moods.

*

I'll give you what for

I'm going to punish or scold you. Seems to stem from the usual response to a threat of punishment - 'What for?' Popular from the late 1800's to 1950's. Origin obscure and is widely used in Britain.

*

I'm on the rattler

I'm on the train. Use when answering your mobile phone in the quiet carriage, at least it might bring a smile to the wearied listeners.

*

Deff it / Deaf it

Forget it. I have heard this expression used in Birmingham for fifty years but still don't know how it is spelt or where it comes from.

*

Ten arf

It is very – as in 'ten arf cold aint it'*

*

I'll ave arf

A half of your finest ale please barman.

*

Ee Ar

I'm giving you this.

*

Got arse in hands

Someone who is angry. Seems to be a local phrase
but there are many variations on the word 'arse' being
used in sayings including for denoting anger, for
example 'arsey'.

*

A right bell oilin

A good beating. Black Country.

*

Cowin

An emphasizing word, substituting for a swear word.
As in Jasper Carrot's famous one liner 'Carrot they
ain't got no Cowin Bovril' in the Blues at Old
Trafford sketch. Origin obscure but there is some
suggestion that 'cowing' means farting in public, as
cows are famously flatulent.

I'm on a line

I'm angry, exasperated or fed up with someone. This seems to be a genuine Brummie term and I can find no information on its origin elsewhere. Me Nan said it all the time, usually at me.

*

A bugger up the back / Little bugger

A little devil or nuisance. The origins of the phrases are thankfully lost in the mists of time and perhaps they should remain so.

*

Can't be arsed

Can't be bothered. Widespread in the UK, and murky in origin. Can't be arsed to investigate further.

*

Daft Apath

You stupid person, but actually has a certain fondness

about it in Birmingham, so tends to be applied to a loved one. Originally Northern, and the 'apeth' is a shortening of 'halfpenny'.

*

The big Brummie mealtime problem

This can cause mayhem. A Brummie 'Dinnertime' happens in the middle of the day. 'Teatime' is the evening meal. No older Brummie will have any truck with 'lunch', 'supper' or going out for 'dinner' in the evening.

*

A voice like a glede /glead under a door

A glede is an ember, of wood or coal, spat out by a fire. The saying alludes to the screeching sound of one of these scraping on a solid floor when trapped under a door. Black Country.

*

Ee's in his oiltot

He is happy or satisfied. This dates back to when

working men would line their stomachs with a shot of olive oil before drinking, believing it would stop them getting too drunk.

*

Up Town

Going to Birmingham City Centre. Brummies tend to go 'up' everywhere, no-one knows why. The use of 'Town' for the City Centre probably dates from before Birmingham became a City in 1889.

*

S'toim

If pronounced correctly, the average brummie will consult their watch and let you know.

*

Titty Babby

A needy, childlike adult. Probably Southern in origin as 'titty baby', but stamped with Brummie credibility by the change to 'babby'. Actually, 'Babby comes from the Anglo Saxon word 'babben' for baby.

*

Bab

The archetypal Brummmie term of endearment,
usually, but not exclusively said by men to women
and children. See above for 'Babby'.

*

Where's ya bin

No, it's not about dustbins, it means 'where have you
been?'

*

Ta

Thank you very much. A child form, dating from the
18th Century.

*

'Oright', Ow ya doin & 'Tara a bit'

Hello and Adieu, Brummie style, probably the best-
known Birmingham saying, it only works with a true
Brummie accent that can achieve an octave spread in

pitch during vocalising.

*

Codge Up

A poorly done job. Black Country.

**Figure 2 Me Mom with other Cadbury's factory
guides at Bournville, circa 1950s**

PART TWO

ACTIONS

To lamp

Thumping someone. Claimed by the Black Country but actually ancient in origin, possibly deriving from the Norse word 'lemja' to 'lame by beating'.

*

To Wag it

Playing truant. Another ancient phrase which is derived from 'hopping the wagon' in the UK, and later adopted by Australia.

*

To Chobble

To crunch a hard sweet noisily. Generations of Brummie kids have been told, 'stop yer chobblin'.

*

To Scrage

To graze ones skin, usually applied to Brummie kids

and their knees.

*

To Mither

To worry, moan, complain. Very old Northern English dialect, but used widely in Birmingham for generations.

*

To Blart

To cry. May derive from a sheep's 'bleat'.

*

To Gambol

To perform a forward roll. Everyone in Birmingham knows what this is, but few realise that hardly anyone else in Britain knows what it means.

*

To Leg It

To run away as fast as possible. There are many and

varied origins of this generic phrase due to the various meanings of the word 'leg'. For example: a leg of a journey, a leg of a sailing race, the human leg. A more local explanation is the 'walking' of barges through tunnels, although it is difficult to see how this transforms into an evocation of swift movement.

*

To mooch

This has several meanings. To sponge off others, investigate; poke about a bit, skulk around. To pretend poverty or act the miser. There are two possible origins. One an ancient old English word, 'mitch', the other French, 'muchier' – to hide or skulk.

*

To cock a deaf un

Pretend not to hear. Origin obscure.

*

To Doss around

To mess about aimlessly. Different from 'dossing' in respect of sleeping rough which is its more usual usage. Its origin as used in Birmingham seems to be unknown. Also used in this way for the phrase **'a right Doss',** meaning something that is either really easy or requires no effort, e.g. 'This job is a right doss'.

*

To Slummock

To move around in an untidy or slovenly fashion. Origin unknown, but at least mid 19th century.

*

To pither / pithering about

To mess about, prevaricate. This seems to be only known in the Midlands and has no obvious other origin. There is a Staffordshire dialect word 'pother', which has a similar meaning.

*

To Bomb it

To run or drive very fast. Origin of this usage unknown.

*

To Crash

To share – usually sweets or cigarettes as in 'crash the ash'.

*

To Boff

To emit a noxious fart. Origin not traced.

*

To Podge (In)

To push into a queue. Seems to be a Birmingham usage. The word podge is an old English one for fat.

*

To Trap / Trapping

To walk, to get walking fast, leave – 'let's trap'.

'Must trap'.

*

To Grizzle

To complain or snivel.

*

To be Chuffed

To be happy. A very old word deriving from 'Chuff' which hundreds of years ago meant swollen with fat. At this time only the rich could be fat so being fat became synonymous with being content.

Figure 3 Me Brummie Nan in er pinny

PART THREE

DESCRIPTIVE WORDS

Miskin (men)

The dustbin / dustbin men. Derives from an old Midlands word 'mixen', which means dungheap or 'midden'.

*

The Buzz

The local **Wumpty,** (West Midlands Passenger Transport Executive) omnibus, the best known of which is the Number 11, 'Outer Circle'.

*

Gassin

Gossiping, chatting, usually used when there are other things to do.

*

Suff

A drain. Claimed by the Black Country and Staffordshire. Common usage in the past in Birmingham.

*

An Island (Traffic)

A roundabout. You may think that everyone calls them 'islands' but try using that when giving directions to a Southerner.

*

Argy–Bargy

An argument. An old English word deriving from the older Scottish, 'Argle–Bargle'.

*

Greebo

A 'greaser'or biker type. Probably from a shortening of the slang 'greaser', which in turn stemmed from the (usually correct) belief that motorcyclists were always covered in oil and grease, - and those that rode

British bikes usually were.

*

Bobowler or Bob Howler

A big hairy moth. Probably Black Country, but an old Birmingham word in usage.

*

The Horse Road

Widely used in Birmingham to denote the road. Also Black Country 'oss road'. A language memory of pre motor vehicle days.

*

Acky 1-2-3

A Birmingham variant of Hide and Seek, with complex playground rules that require lawyers to unscramble. The 'Acky Post' was where the person 'on' would count up from. If the 'hiders' got back to the Post without being touched and shouted 'Acky 123' they were safe. I think......

*

Bostin

Brilliant, great, excellent. Claimed by both Black Country and Brummies and I'm not getting involved. What is beyond dispute is that it is our local Midlands word, not used elsewhere. It may derive from Anglo-Saxon 'bosten', meaning something to boast about. Be proud of it, and use it. (Also the name of our Facebook page *'Bostin Books', please visit and 'like' us*).

*

Our kid / Mom / Dad / Wench / The Nipper/ Nan

The family. 'Mom', not 'Mum' is a Brummie spelling. 'Our Kid' seems to be Brummie, but 'Our Wench' is Black Country. Brummies report being called 'the Nipper' from childhood through to their Seventies. Origin unknown. Nan is Grandma of course, we didn't have enough 'ackers' for Nannies.

*

Yampy / Barmy / Barmpot

Mad, Crazy. Black Country. The 16th Century word, 'Barm', means frothing and excitable. 'Balmy' in the

1800's meant 'foolish'.

*

A piece / A bad (h)and

A slice of bread (and butter), or a sandwich. As in, 'If you behave you'll get a jam piece' A 'bad (h)and' is somewhat obscure but seems to denote a jam doorstop.

*

The Outdoor

The Off–Licence or 'Offie'. A few Birmingham pubs actually had a signed 'Outdoor' attached to them.

*

A Cob

A bun, crusty or not. We could spend a lot of time on this – but we won't.

*

Snap

Food, can also mean a food break when working e.g.

'Snap–time'. Common Birmingham Police usage –
'book me in for snap'.

*

The Cut

The Canal - Black Country. I presume it stems from
the canals being 'cut' out of the ground. 'Up the cut'
means to go along the towpath, 'In the cut' is where
the shopping trolleys go.

*

Cack-Handed

Clumsy, not dexterous with hands, can't wipe their
backside properly. Can also mean left–handed and is
linked to the Black Country 'cag-handed', which
means left – handed. The word 'cack' is 15th Century
Old English, meaning to void excrement, which in
turn comes from 'cacare', Latin for 'to defecate'.

*

Arf / Half– Soaked

Dozy, forgetful, slow-witted. A 'soak' is an old word

for a drunk.

*

Sterra

Sterilised Milk, beloved of Bummies and delivered to the doorstep in bottles.

*

Fizzog

The face. The word is a slang version of 'physiognomy' - the facial features.

*

The Bog / Lar Pom

The Toilet. It is alleged that 'Lar Pom' stems from the Victorian habit of not referring directly to bodily functions, so a posh-sounding word based on the French 'La Pomme' – Apple was used. While we are on this subject the **'Gazzunda'** was the chamber pot because it goes under the bed.

*

Cake-Hole

The mouth. Black Country.

*

Gansey or Ganzey

A pullover. Comes from the word 'Guernsey' which is obvious when you think about it – it's near to 'Jersey'.

*

Pikelet

A type of crumpet. I kid you not, there are pages about how it's cooked and how it differs from crumpets and muffins and this book is too short for that. The word apparently comes from Wales where a 'Bara -Pyglyd' is a type of spongy /'pitchy' bread. Any road up, we used to have them toasted in front of the gas fire then smothered in butter.

*

Gully & Entry

A Gully in this context is a narrow street or

passageway. It comes from 'gullet' / gorge which indicates narrowing, as of the throat. Interestingly, in Hindi, 'Gully' means a street and I wonder whether the Days of The Raj have some connection with the term. An Entry is the alleyway between terraced houses.

*

Kaylied / Kaylie

This is a complicated one. Kaylie is a type of sherbert, not the powder type but crystalline, usually eaten by dipping a stick of liquorice into it. It may or may not have originated from a shortening of 'alkali' but no-one seems to know for sure.

*

'Kaylied' is a Midlands term for being drunk. It is no doubt a convoluted linkage between the slang word 'sherbert' meaning alcohol, usually beer, and Kaylie. The best pronunciation is Brummie where it sounds like 'Kayloy'.

*

Donnies

Hands – usually children's. 'Put ya gloves on yer donnies'. 'Clean yer Donnies and you'll get a piece'. Allegedly comes from the French 'Donez', 'to give'. How it got into usage in Birmingham is anyone's guess.

*

Gormless

Stupid. An ancient word, 'gaum', meaning 'understanding', that in turn derives from The Norse 'gaumr' meaning 'care or heed'.

*

Reeky / Ronk /Riffy

Smelly or dirty. 'Reeky' derives from the Old English 'reac' – smoking, which had changed by the 1700s to mean smelling bad. Famously used by Shakespeare, *'the breath that from my mistress reeks'*, and he also used it to imply something that is suspicious or 'fishy'. 'Ronk' is a Northern word that probably combines 'rotten' and 'stink'. 'Riffy' seems to be Black Country.

Reasty

Food that's gone off. Dirty. Black Country.

*

Trankelments

Small possessions, ornaments or paraphernalia. Black Country. Also claimed by Yorkshire.

*

Gawping

To stare open–mouthed in wonder. Origin the Old English word 'Gielpan', to boast, which is related to 14th Century 'galpen', to gape or yawn.

*

Rocks

Sweets. Often linked with the verb 'to crash', 'crash the rocks mate'. Can also be 'chobbled' vigorously.

*

Adams Ale

Pure water. All that Adam had to drink in the Garden of Eden. First written usage 1643, and became very popular within the Temperance movement in the 19th Century.

*

Fizzy Pop

As opposed to just 'pop', which is ordinary squash – without the bubbles. The fizzy stuff came via door-to-door delivery from the Alpine or Corona pop man, and I liked Dandelion and Burdock best.

*

A Benny

A slow or dull-witted person. A fairly modern piece of Brummie slang that relates to the character 'Benny', from the Midlands TV soap, 'Crossroads'.

*

Tip Tops and Jubbly's

Flavoured blocks of ice for kids, beloved of

Brummies. A 'Tip Top' was a long thin one, the 'Jubbly' was a triangular / pyramidal shape. A good sucking usually extracted all the flavouring leaving a lump of ice that could often be put down the back of the unwary.

*

Jasper

A Wasp. Was in widespread British usage. It is thought to date back to at least medieval times and to be derived from the latin for a Wasp – 'vespa'.

*

Gamgee

Cotton wool. Joseph Gamgee was a surgeon at Birmingham General Hospital and in 1880 invented 'Gamgee Tissue', an absorbent cotton wool and gauze dressing. The name directly inspired J.R.R Tolkein to name Frodo Baggins' faithful companion, 'Sam Gamgee' in 'The Lord of The Rings'.

*

Jacksy

Not the Cockney one meaning backside. Ours means
lucky, as in 'you jacksy bastard'.

*

Marlies

Either the game of marbles or the normal size
marbles. The big ones were called 'Gobbies'. This
seems to be a Midlands word.

*

Scrap

A fight. Probably derived from the old word 'scrape'.

*

Scraps and Bits

Leftover batter served with chips. Also called
'batterbits'.

*

Nunk

Nothing. No indication of origin.

*

Arly-Barley

A request for truce or surrender. Part of the
playground game, Acky 123, but used by adults too.
May stem from French, 'Allez Parler' (Go and talk).

*

Tatered

Tired. Can mean intoxicated but generally in
Birmingham is used for fatigued, especially by the
older population.

*

Mickey Mouse

A pint of Bitter and Lager mixed half and half.

*

Brown and Mild

A pint of Mild Beer, (Ansells or M&B), with a bottle of Mann's Stout.

*

Gnat's knacker

A unit of measurement used in Brummie engineering.

*

The Rezza

The Reservoir.

*

Bint

A girl. Comes from the identical Arabic word, meaning daughter or girl. Brought back to the UK after the British occupation of Egypt at the end of the 19th Century.

*

Garding

The Brummie garden.

*

The Garage

The Petrol Station.

*

Tig

The Brummie version of 'Tag', the children's game. *

*

Dollop

A large shapeless mass – usually used in connection with food. A 16th Century English word that in turn comes from a Scandinavian word, probably 'dolp' which is Norwegian for 'lump'.

*

Cogwinder

A punch. A clout round the ear. Black Country.

*

Council Pop

Tapwater.

*

The Ostin

'The Austin', the legendary car company of Birmingham, manufacturer of such fine vehicles as the Austin Allegro. Later 'British Leyland', and now, unfortunately gone, the sad remnants owned by Shanghai Automotive.

*

Ackers

Money. Claimed as Cockney slang, but more likely brought back from Egypt by British troops as is from the Arabic 'akka' which means a coin worth one piastre.

*

A note from the authors

If you enjoyed this book, please leave a review on its Amazon page. It will be much appreciated. If you want to know more about our Brummie / Midlands books, fiction and non – fiction, please visit and 'like' our Facebook Page, 'Bostin Books'. I hope you enjoy them. Tara for now.

Stephen Burrows (& Michael Layton).

February 2018

Printed in Poland
by Amazon Fulfillment
Poland Sp. z o.o., Wrocław

51052588R00031